# LOOK INSIDE

# Computer

Catherine Chambers

Heinemann Interactive Library
Des Plaines, Illinois

Designed by Celia Floyd
Printed in Hong Kong
02 01 00 99 98
10 9 8 7 6 5 4 3 2 1

**Library of Congress Cataloging-in-Publication Data**
Chambers, Catherine, 1954-
        Computer / Catherine Chambers.
            p.    cm. — (Look inside)
        Includes bibliographical references and index.
        Summary: Simple text and detailed photographs look inside computers, describe their components, and explain how to use them.
        ISBN 1-57572-622-X (lib. bdg.)
        1. Computer—Juvenile literature.    [1. Computers.]    I. Title.
    II. Series: Chambers, Catherine, 1954-    Look inside.
        QA76.23.C48      1998
        004-dc21                                           97-31456
                                                            CIP
                                                            AC

**Acknowledgments**
The publisher would like to thank the following for permission to reproduce photographs: Anthony King/Medimage, pp. 4–12, 14–16, 18–21; Science Photo Library, p. 13 (Nelson Morris), p. 17 (Thomas Porett)

Cover photograph: Chris Honeywell

Our thanks to Betty Root for her comments in the preparation of this book and to Apricot for their assistance.

Every effort has been made to contact copyright holders of any material reproduced in this book. Any omissions will be rectified in subsequent printings if notice is given to the publisher.

"For Richard"

Some words are shown in bold, **like this**. You can find out what they mean by looking in the glossary.

# CONTENTS

# HERE'S A COMPUTER

All these bits and pieces make up the parts of
a computer. You can see many shapes and sizes.
There are strong boxes. There are long, **flexible**
wires called cables. You can see different
materials, too. Some are hard. Others are soft.

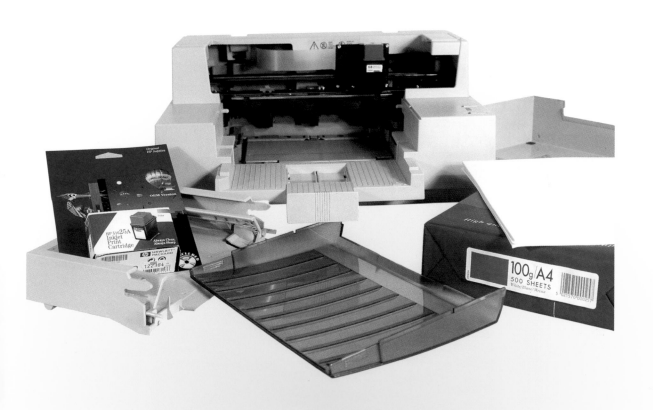

Some parts give the computer information. These are called the input. Other parts work things out. These are the processors. Other parts store information. These are called the memory. The pieces that show all the work are the output.

# THE KEYBOARD

The keyboard is part of the input. It is used to type information into the computer through a **circuit board**. The keyboard is made mostly from tough plastic. It is thin and lies flat. This keeps your hands and wrists from hurting when you type.

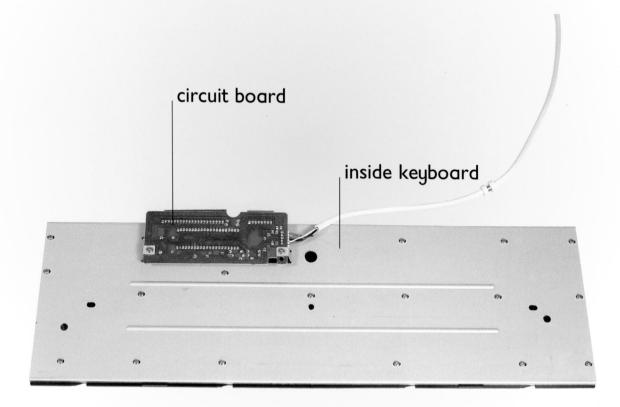

circuit board

inside keyboard

The keys are close together. Your fingers can reach all the keys easily. There is a soft spring underneath each key. It lets the key up quickly, so typing is faster. A long cable leads to the computer.

leads to computer

keys

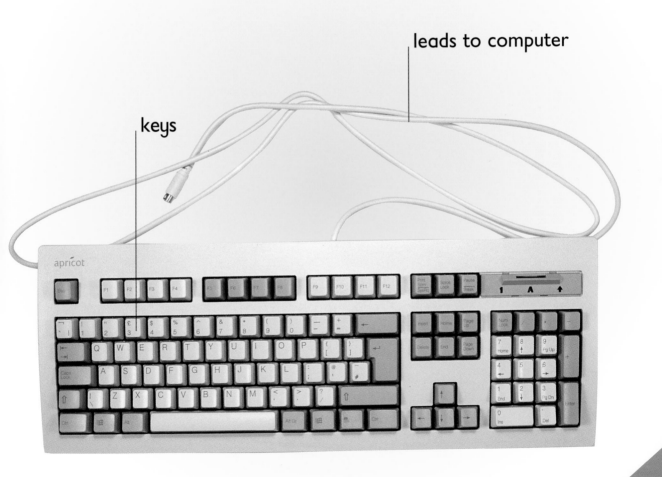

# THE MOUSE

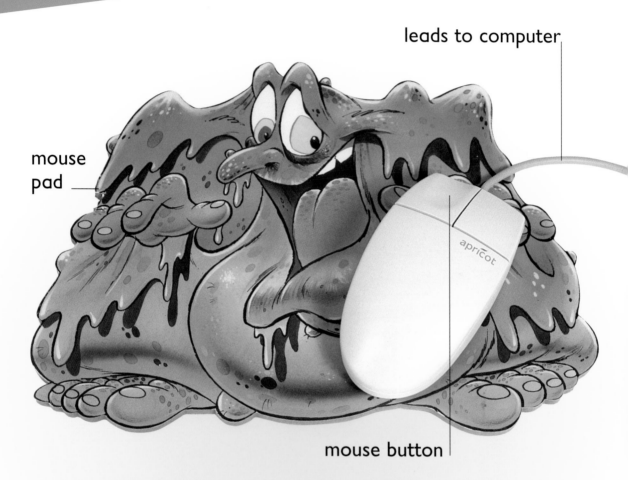

leads to computer

mouse pad

mouse button

The mouse is also part of the input. It helps you to find and show things on the computer screen. You click a button at the front to find what you need. There is a soft spring underneath the mouse button.

Inside the mouse, there are rollers and a ball. These help you move the mouse in any direction. The mouse **glides** on smooth plastic runners. Its shape makes it easy to hold.

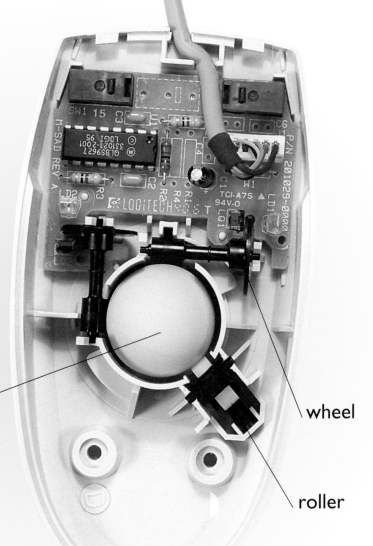

leads to computer

ball

wheel

roller

# THE CPU

The C.P.U., or Central Processing Unit, is a rectangular plastic box. It holds the main processor. This is like the computer's brain. It figures things out. The C.P.U. also holds the hard drive. This stores information—it's part of the memory. A metal box protects the hard drive.

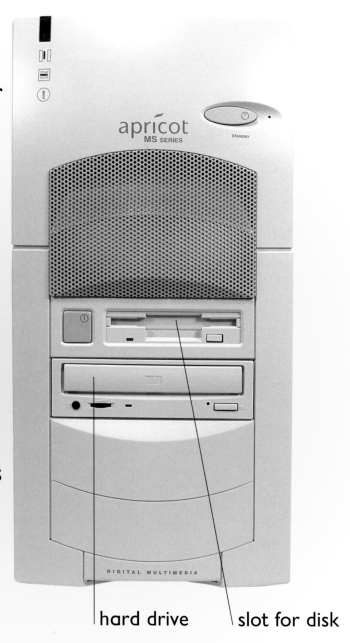

hard drive    slot for disk

The C.P.U. has a narrow slot in it. This is called the disk drive. It holds floppy disks. These disks give information to the main processor. An **electronic magnet** lies inside the disk drive. It reads the information on the disk. This is passed on to the main processor chip.

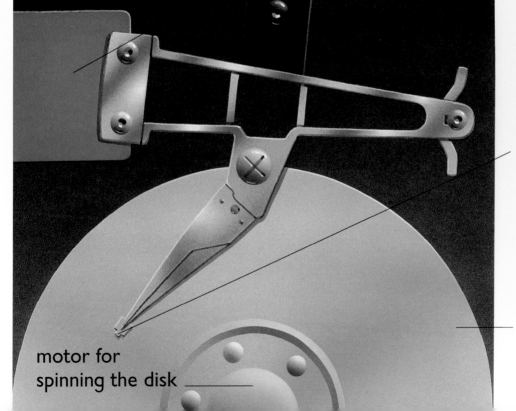

motor for moving magnetic head

magnetic head for reading the disk

disk

motor for spinning the disk

# CHIPS

The main processor is made up of chips and hundreds of wires. It contains thousands of switches. These control the flow of **electric signals**. The chips sort and store millions of pieces of information. They work out instructions given by computer programs.

plastic block

**silicon** chips
(smaller processors)

cooler (heat sink) covering the main processor

A chip is made of a thin slice of silicon. Tiny electronic parts are put into each slice in layers. The silicon is protected by a plastic case. Metal strips connect the chip to other parts of the computer.

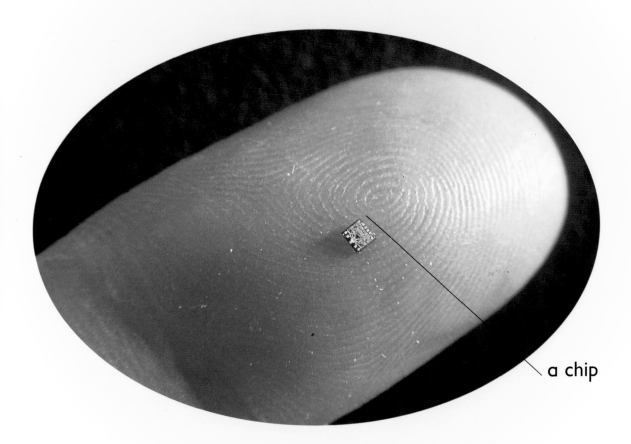

a chip

# FLOPPY DISKS

A floppy disk holds information. It is part of the computer's memory. It also gives information to the main processor. It is part of the input.

disk label

hard plastic disk case

DOUBLE DENSITY
MFD-2DD

Fonts
Version 1.0

English

The disk is made of floppy, shiny plastic. It is coated with tiny pieces of **magnetized** material that hold the information. The disk is delicate. It is protected by a metal shield and has a hard plastic case as well.

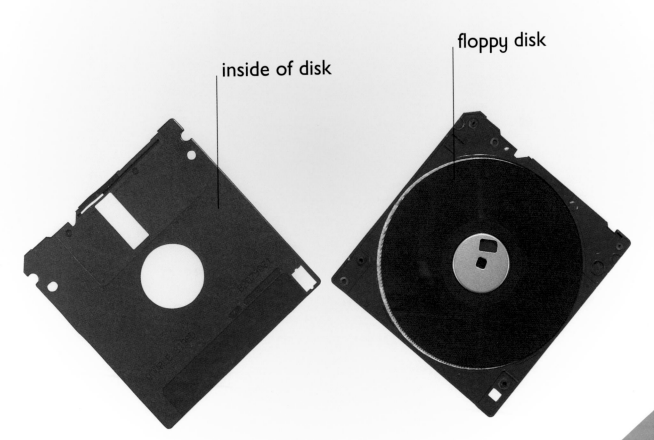

inside of disk

floppy disk

# THE PRINTER

This box is another output machine. It is an inkjet printer. The computer's electronic messages get printed as words and pictures. The signals are sent along thin copper wires. The wires are inside a clear plastic strip.

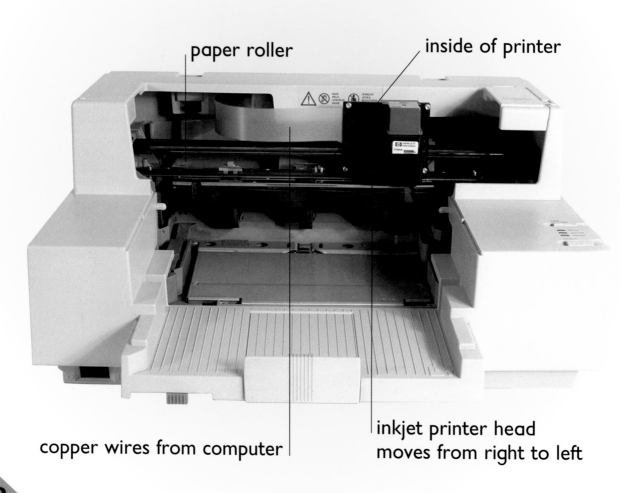

paper roller

inside of printer

inkjet printer head moves from right to left

copper wires from computer

The **flexible** plastic strip moves with the print head and the ink holder. They slide together across the paper. The paper moves along metal rollers. It is pushed forward as each jet of color is printed.

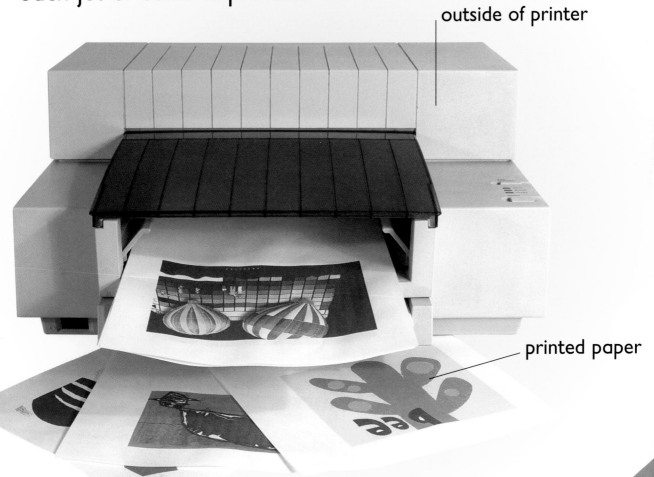

outside of printer

printed paper

# USING A COMPUTER

Here are the computer parts. They are protected in strong plastic boxes. The parts are connected with **flexible** cables and plug into an electric power supply. Cables connect the boxes to each other, too.

The computer parts are placed near each other. This makes it easy to use each piece. The screen needs to be at eye level. Notice the plain colors of the pieces. Bright colors might keep you from concentrating on your work!

# GLOSSARY

**circuit board**   board with tiny switches and wires that control the flow of signals from one part of a machine to another

**electric signals**   messages produced by electricity

**electronic magnet**   magnet made by passing electricity through wire

**flexible**   bends easily

**glides**   moves smoothly

**magnetized**   made magnetic

**silicon**   type of non-metal rock that can be made into very thin layers

# MORE BOOKS TO READ

Children's Press. *Computers: Personal Computers.*
Children's Press, 1997.

Kinkoph, Sherry. *Alpha-Bytes Fun With Computers.*
Indianapolis, Ind: Alpha Books, 1992.

Wright, David. *Computers.* Tarrytown, NY:
Marshall Cavendish, 1995.

# INDEX